PENGUI

BOOK OF HAIKUS

JACK KEROUAC was born in Lowell, Massachusetts, in 1922, the youngest of three children in a Franco-American family. He attended local Catholic and public schools and won a football scholarship to Columbia University in New York City, where he met Allen Ginsberg and William S. Burroughs. His first novel, *The Town and the City*, appeared in 1950, but it was *On the Road*, first published in 1957, that made Kerouac one of the most controversial and best-known writers of his time. Publication of his many other books followed, among them *The Subterraneans*, *Big Sur*, and *The Dharma Bums*, in which he describes his discovery of haiku. Kerouac's books of poetry include *Mexico City Blues*, *Scattered Poems*, *Pomes All Sizes*, *Heaven and Other Poems*, and *Book of Blues*. Kerouac died in St. Petersburg, Florida, in 1969, at the age of forty-seven.

REGINA WEINREICH teaches in the Department of Humanities and Sciences at the School of Visual Arts in New York and has published widely in periodicals including *The New York Times*, *The Review of Contemporary Fiction*, *The Washington Post*, *The Boston Globe*, *The Village Voice*, and in the literary journals *The Paris Review* and *Five Points*. She is the author of *Kerouac's Spontaneous Poetics: A Study of the Fiction*. She was a writer on the documentary *The Beat Generation: An American Dream* and a producer/director of *Paul Bowles: The Complete Outsider*.

by Jack Kerouac

Jack Kerouac

BOOK
OF
HAIKUS

Edited and with an Introduction by
Regina Weinreich

Penguin Poets

PENGUIN BOOKS
Published by the Penguin Group
Penguin Group (USA) Inc., 375 Hudson Street, New York, New York 10014, U.S.A.
Penguin Group (Canada), 90 Eglinton Avenue East, Suite 700, Toronto,
Ontario, Canada M4P 2Y3 (a division of Pearson Penguin Canada Inc.)
Penguin Books Ltd, 80 Strand, London WC2R 0RL, England
Penguin Ireland, 25 St Stephen's Green, Dublin 2, Ireland
(a division of Penguin Books Ltd)
Penguin Group (Australia), 250 Camberwell Road, Camberwell, Victoria 3124, Australia
(a division of Pearson Australia Group Pty Ltd)
Penguin Books India Pvt Ltd, 11 Community Centre, Panchsheel Park,
New Delhi – 110 017, India
Penguin Group (NZ), 67 Apollo Drive, Rosedale, North Shore 0632, New Zealand
(a division of Pearson New Zealand Ltd)
Penguin Books (South Africa) (Pty) Ltd, 24 Sturdee Avenue,
Rosebank, Johannesburg 2196, South Africa

Penguin Books Ltd, Registered Offices: 80 Strand, London WC2R 0RL, England

First published in Penguin Books 2003

LIBRARY OF CONGRESS CATALOGING-IN-PUBLICATION DATA
Kerouac, Jack, 1922–1969
Book of haikus / Jack Kerouac ; edited and with an introduction by Regina Weinreich.
p. cm.
Includes bibliographical references.
ISBN 978-0-14-200264-3
1. Haiku, American. 2. Nature—Poetry. I. Weinreich, Regina, 1949–. II. Title.
PS3521.E735 B66 2003
811'.54—dc21 2002032269

Printed in the United States of America
Set in New Caledonia and Twentieth Century • Designed by Sabrina Bowers

Contents

Various themes — first
Carver flute, then Poet
Trombones, then mention
of Ma's Oboe, then
Burroughs' Drum etc

—

The bird of Spring
died early

The old man
woke
— The lady
died

Then I'll invent
  The American Haiku type:
  The simple rhyming triolet:—
Seventeen syllables?
No, as I say, American Pops:—
Simple 3-line poems

Reading Notes 1965

Introduction:
The Haiku Poetics of
Jack Kerouac

The American writer Jack Kerouac is mostly known as a prose fiction stylist. He is famous for his bestselling novel *On the Road* and for having spawned the Beat Generation. For some, images of rebellious hipsters come to mind, as well as a beat determination not to revise, first thought best thought. But careful readers of Kerouac's prose recognize that within the ragged, circular, soulful cadences for which his writing is at once criticized, imitated and revered is the rhythmic phrasing of poetry.

Among the literati who knew him best, Jack Kerouac was a poet supreme who worked in several poetry traditions, including sonnets, odes, psalms, and blues (which he based on blues and jazz idioms). He also successfully adapted haiku into English, his "American haikus."[1] "'Haiku,'" he wrote, "was invented and developed over hundreds of years in Japan to be a complete poem in seventeen syllables and to pack in a whole vision of life in three short lines." Finding that Western languages cannot adapt themselves to the "fluid syllabillic Japanese," he sought to redefine the genre:

"I propose that the 'Western Haiku' simply say a lot in three short lines in any Western language. Above all, a Haiku must be very simple and free of all poetic trickery and make a little picture and yet be as airy and graceful as a Vivaldi Pas-

---

1. Haiku is both singular and plural. Kerouac's usage of "*s*" is unusual. Ginsberg retains the same usage, except in his *Paris Review* interview, where editing may have occurred.

torella. Here is a great Japanese Haiku that is simpler and prettier than any Haiku I could ever write in any language:—

A day of quiet gladness,—
   Mount Fuji is veiled
In misty rain.   (Bashō) (1644–1694)

Thus, in this tradition, Kerouac wrote:

Birds singing
   in the dark
Rainy dawn

Kerouac composed this and hundreds more haiku in notebooks dated from 1956 to 1966. These small, bound notebooks—the kind he could press into his checkered lumberman's shirt pocket and carry around anywhere for fresh and spontaneous entries—contain a huge cache of his three-line jottings, a mother lode, so to speak, from which he selected what would comprise his Book of Haikus, a collection he urged Lawrence Ferlinghetti to publish in 1961. Five Working Notebooks dated 1961–1965 are another source of haiku, and more were em-

bedded in novels, letters, or published in small literary maga-
zines. Twenty-six, some chosen for a 1964 anthology of Amer-
ican verse edited by his Italian translator, Fernanda Pivano,
were published posthumously in 1971 by City Lights in *Scat-
tered Poems*. A manuscript page (Berg Collection of the New
York Public Library) indicates Kerouac's intentions.

Jack Kerouac was not the first American poet to experiment in
haiku aesthetics. Before him, Ezra Pound, William Carlos
Williams, Amy Lowell, and Wallace Stevens all created haiku-
inspired verse. It was not until after the Second World War
that a "rigorous and informed attention to the genre"[2] arose,
with the first volume of R. H. Blyth's four-volume *Haiku* ap-
pearing in 1949, bringing the classical traditions of haiku and
Zen to the West.

Kerouac turned to Buddhist study and practice after his

---

2. Tom Lynch's essay "A path toward nature: Haiku's Aesthetics of
   Awareness" provides a historical perspective on the role of haiku
   in American poetry of the twentieth century. See also Rick
   Fields's *How the Swans Came to the Lake: A Narrative History
   of Buddhism in America*.

"road" period, from 1953 until 1956, in the lull between the writing of the seminal *On the Road* in 1951,2 and its publication in 1957—that is, before fame changed everything. When he finished *The Subterraneans* in the fall of 1953, fed up with the world after the failed love affair on which the book was based, he picked up Thoreau and fantasized a life separate from civilization. Then he happened upon Asvaghosha's *The Life of Buddha* and immersed himself in Zen study.

Kerouac began his genre-defying book *Some of the Dharma* in 1953 as a collection of reader's notes on Dwight Goddard's *The Buddhist Bible;* the endeavor grew into a massive compilation of spiritual material, meditations, prayers, and haiku, a study of his musings on the teaching of Buddha. By 1955, while living in North Carolina with his sister, he worked on two other Buddhist-related texts: *Wake Up*, his own biography of the Buddha, and *Buddha Tells Us,* translations of "works done by great Rimbauvian Frenchmen at the Abbeys of Tibet," what he refers to in his letters as "a full length Buddhist Handbook."

Haiku came to the West Coast poets through Gary Snyder. Inspired by D. T. Suzuki's *Essays in Zen Buddhism* (1927) in the fall of 1951, Snyder spent the early '50s traveling in Japan, studying and practicing Zen Buddhism. Philip Whalen and Lew Welch became avid haiku practitioners through his influence. Kerouac, Ginsberg, Snyder, and Whalen spent time together in Berkeley in 1955 talking, drinking, and trading their own versions of Blyth's haiku translations, which they were reading in all four volumes. Through Blyth's translations and his extraordinary commentary on the Japanese works, Kerouac found emotive and aesthetic sympathies. Even though he attempted to meditate, wrote a sutra, "The Scripture of the Golden Eternity" (1956) at Gary Snyder's behest, and thought of his entire oeuvre, his Legend of Duluoz, as a "Divine Comedy" based on Buddha,[3] Buddhism stayed a literary concern for him, not a meditative or spiritual practice, as it was for Snyder and Whalen. Later, when he told Ted Berrigan in his 1968 *Paris Review* interview he was a serious Buddhist, but not a Zen Buddhist, the distinction was to separate his interest from the prevalent scholarly study of dogma in favor of

---

3. Handwritten note on ms. page of poem "Daydreams for Ginsberg," February 10, 1955, Rare Books and Manuscripts Library, Columbia University.
4. Jack Kerouac, *Paris Review* interview, pp. 84–5.

Buddhist essence.[4] The practice of haiku, however, persisted throughout his life, becoming an important medium for rendering the Beat ideal of "shapely mind," and for crafting an American Mysticism in the manner of Thoreau. For a new generation of poets, Kerouac ended up breaking ground at a pioneering stage of an American haiku movement.

Finding these haiku was a bit like extracting gold from baser metals, so embedded were many of them (nearly 1,000) in blocks of prose, scribble, and even street addresses. Many reappear throughout his work, because Kerouac recycled his haiku, using them in different ways.

Traditional haiku collections are organized by season or subject, but that did not seem an appropriate way to present Kerouac's haiku. Part I of this volume is comprised of haiku he selected himself. The chronological organization of the haiku in Part II seemed the best way to give a sense of the evolution of the work, as well as to see each poem in its own light. Handy for this approach, Kerouac, in a 1963 journal, divided up his life according to the seasonal haiku reference, and so, following his idea, I have taken Spring and Summer as the period before the publication of *On the Road,* Autumn and Winter as after, in his later years.[5]

This book endeavors to include examples of the entire range of Kerouac's haiku—those which he selected for publication (The Book of Haikus found in a black folder so named) and poems in those subcategories by which he experimented in haiku possibilities: the philosophical "pops" as well as the angry, emotionally blunt "beat generation haikus." As with all of Kerouac's work in prose and poetry, process is key to his search for more refined language.

Allen Ginsberg spoke perhaps hyperbolically of Kerouac as the "only *master* of the haiku: He's the only one in the United States who knows how to write haiku . . . [he] talks that way, thinks that way."[6] What Kerouac "got" perhaps more than any other Beat poet working in this genre was the rendering of a

---

5. See *Selected Letters 1957–1969,* p. 355. "ROAD was learned in my Springtime, & prepared incredible work of Summer (CODY, SAX, MAGGIE, SUBS, GERARD, ANGELS etc.). . . . Then came Autumn, to which BIG SUR belongs & all my present unhappy exhaustion of harvest time--for next 10 years I'll be harvesting & winnowing chaffs but with no great mindless purpose of summer—" (excerpt from journal entry).
6. Allen Ginsberg, *Paris Review* interview, pp. 66–7.

subject's essence, and the shimmering, ephemeral nature of its fleeting existence. This sensitivity to impermanence appears again and again in his work, from *The Town and the City*, constructed around the death of the father, through *The Book of Dreams*, which evokes the frail individual beset with a harsh, indifferent society, at times succumbing, defeated.

One of Kerouac's classic haiku images is of a sole animate entity in a wide, cavernous expanse:

> The windmills of
>   Oklahoma look
> In every direction

And, from a 1960 notebook:

> One flower
>   on the cliffside
> Nodding at the canyon

That isolated being—here "look[ing]" or "nodding"—is the quintessential Kerouacean persona seen again and again in his Legend of Duluoz.

Seeking visual possibilities in language, Kerouac combined his spontaneous prose with sketching, a technique suggested to him by Ed White, a friend during his Columbia University days in the late '40s: Why don't you sketch in the streets like a painter but with words?

"'Keep the eye STEADILY on the object,' for haiku," he exhorted himself in his notebooks. "WRITE HAIKUS THEN PAINT THE SCENE DESCRIBING THEM!" He also likened good haiku to good painting. The best haiku gave him "the sensation I get looking at a great painting by Van Gogh, it's there & nothing you can say or do about it, except *look* in dismay at the power of looking."

Kerouac also recognized the purposeful caesura or cut of Japanese haiku as key to its sound and sense. Quoting Shakespeare in a 1963 Notebook, Kerouac wrote: "birds sit brooding in the snow' (combining the thought as well as the sound of the ellipse of a JAP *haiku*) always wondered where did he get that sound? & always think, that's what I like about S, where he revels in the great world night." The extraordinary juxtapositions often noted in Kerouac's sketched prose—in *Visions of Cody* (written in 1951 and 1952, a portion published in 1959 as *Visions of Neal*), *Doctor Sax* (written in July

1952, published in 1959), and "October in the Railroad Earth," (1952)—especially evoke haiku spirit, even before he was fully immersed in composing haiku.

As indicated in letters, journals, and especially in his *Paris Review* interview, where he playfully appears not to have a clue, Kerouac was insecure about his own haiku abilities. "Haiku is best reworked and revised,"[7] he told his interviewers. As lack of revision, or lack of writerly control, has been consistently used to criticize Kerouac's work, his insistence on revision for haiku should go against the charge that his writing is mere mindless rebellion. Kerouac's notebooks show haiku composition as a matter of discipline, as difficult to achieve as spending time in Zen meditation.

The discovery of haiku through Dr. Suzuki's work and Blyth's translations is the starting point of *The Dharma Bums*. The struggle to perfect haiku becomes part of the narrative motif in this novel, published in 1958, and dedicated to Han Shan,

7. Kerouac, *Paris Review* interview, p. 104.

the Chinese poet whose work Snyder was translating.[8] Calling his mentor Gary Snyder "Japhy Ryder" in his slant rhyme, Kerouac has this nature boy/Zen mystic/poet supplant the speedy Dean Moriarty of *On the Road* as catalyst for the Kerouac persona, this time named Ray Smith, in learning the ways of "dharma bums."

In the course of the novel the two decide to go mountain-climbing, Japhy as Virgil to Ray's Dante. They engage in a sharing of poetry, observation of nature, and speculation on haiku practice. Says Smith, perusing a fresh pure lake, "by god it's a haiku in itself."

"'Look over there,' sang Japhy, 'yellow aspens. Just put me

---

8. Kerouac became aware of the Chinese poet Han Shan (A.D. 700–780), a contemporary of Li Po, through Snyder's Cold Mountain translations. Han Shan was famously reclusive, and there is no small comparison between his life on the mountain and Kerouac's sojourn on Desolation Peak. Cold Mountain is where Han Shan lived, but it also refers to himself and his state of mind. All that is known of him is that he was poor, looked like a tramp, and was thought to be crazy. See "Preface to the Poems of Han-Shan by Lu Ch'iu-yin, Governor of T'ai Prefecture" in *The Gary Snyder Reader*.

in the mind of a haiku. . . . Talking about the literary life—the yellow aspens.' Walking in this country you could understand the perfect gems of haikus the Oriental poets had written, never getting drunk in the mountains or anything but just going along as fresh as children writing down what they saw without literary devices or fanciness of expression. We made up haikus as we climbed, winding up and up now on the slopes of brush.

"'Rocks on the side of the cliff,' I said, 'why don't they tumble down?'

"'Maybe that's a haiku, maybe not, it might be a little too complicated,' said Japhy. 'A real haiku's gotta be as simple as porridge and yet make you see the real thing, like the greatest haiku of them all probably is the one that goes "The sparrow hops along the veranda, with wet feet." By Shiki. You see the wet footprints like a vision in your mind and yet in those few words you also see the rain that's been falling that day and almost smell the wet pine needles.'"

As Kerouac's fictionalized account makes clear, his original sources go back to the Japanese artists as he read them in

Blyth: Matsuo Bashō (1644–1694), who brought together the small and transient elements of nature with its vast ones; Yosa Buson (1716–1784), who brought a painter's perspective to poetry; Kobayashi Issa (1762–1826), who wrote more psychologically resonant poems, deeply affected by the tragic early death of his mother; and Masaoka Shiki (1867–1902), who favored sketching from life.

Blyth's helpful commentary gave Kerouac a window into the gestalt and very culture of haiku, the thusness and suchness, the traditional tropes: the seasons, wind, night, dusk, dawn, mist, birds, crickets, the moon and the stars, all are interwoven with his own contemporary concerns. Kerouac's techniques related to haiku traditions might explain why, despite so many misfires and imperfect passes at haiku, Kerouac nevertheless is well regarded among today's American haiku poets.

Given that his mind-set, though akin to the Japanese artists' sensibilities, is yet miles and years apart, and that his aesthetic, highly refined in its own sense, comes truly from another world, Kerouac does at times achieve a depth and richness approaching that of his models:

Useless! useless!
　—heavy rain driving
Into the sea

This lament on man's endeavors, futile against the inevitability of Nature, evokes the timeless and universal spirit of the Japanese poets. In other haiku, his sensibility—the process by which language comes to him, and that distinctly Kerouacean idiom that allows for the reduction of language to babble at times—more fully dominates. Kerouac used place names, real and imagined, people's names, and abstractions such as eternity and the Void as markers, in much the same way as the Japanese poets used the seasons, flora and fauna, to invoke mood.

A mix of Japanese and Western ideals is also seen in Kerouac's "Blues and Haikus" collection, recorded with Al Cohn and Zoot Sims. Here Kerouac successfully blended "melancholy with the world-weariness of blues tradition."[9] A 1957 notebook records his assertion that "Poetry is meant to be

---

9. Tom Lynch, "A Way of Awareness: The Emerging Delineaments of American Haiku" (unpublished essay).

sung to music"; overall, the 1959 recording responds to a different instinct from that of the Japanese models. And yet, "Crossing the football field/coming home from work/the lonely businessman" and "The barn, swimming/in a sea/Of wind-blown leaves"—are well attuned to both, a fusion of traditional haiku and Western bluesy tones.

Haiku Prose

Kerouac's use of haiku was not limited to poetry. Reviewing *The Dharma Bums* in *The Village Voice* on November 12, 1958, Ginsberg noted that: "The sentences are shorter (shorter than the great flowing inventive *Dr. Sax*), almost as if he were writing a book of a thousand *haikus*. . . . *Dharma Bums* winds up with a great series of perfectly connected associations in visionary *haikus* (little jumps of the "freedom of eternity"). (Two images set side by side that make a flash in the mind.) Kerouac too saw that leap:

A sentence that's short and sweet with a sudden jump of thought is a kind of haiku, and there's a lot of freedom and fun in surprising yourself with that, let the mind willy-nilly jump from the branch to the bird.[10]

Haiku seeps into his prose style in other ways. In *The Dharma Bums,* he writes, "The storm went away as swiftly as it came and the late afternoon lake-sparkle blinded me. Late afternoon, my mop drying on the rock. Late afternoon, my bare back cold as I stood above the world in a snowfield digging shovelsful into a pail. Late afternoon, it was I not the void that changed." The repetitive "late afternoon" sequence—Kerouac's "visionary haikus" here written out as prose phrases—echoes the manner in which he wrote haiku in his journals, often repeating a line with a variation. These "late afternoon" haiku also appear in #1 of his pocket notebooks marked "Desolation Peak 1956." Handwritten, they follow the three-line haiku form and are not consecutive. Several of these are also included in a 1956 typed haiku manuscript consisting of seventy-two numbered poems, which he dubbed "Desolation Pops."

Kerouac's linguistic alchemy is shown in his prose transformation of the haiku in *Trip Trap: Haiku along the Road from*

---

10. Kerouac, *Paris Review* interview, p. 117.

San Francisco to New York (1959, published posthumously in 1973). A collaboration with his friends Lew Welch and Albert Saijo, this slim volume is a record of three guys amusing one another by tossing off haiku in a one-upmanship game that captures the passing landscape from a moving car. For a 1963 travel piece for *Holiday Magazine,* Kerouac improves upon the sillier haiku variants of the earlier publication:

> Oklahoma—in any direction flat, pure, quiet. Cows rushing like dots as tho they were as far away as Nebraska. Grain elevators waiting for the farmers to come home from church. Grain elevators, like tall trucks waiting for the road to approach them. Radio antennae hard to see somewhere. . . . Windmills looking in every direction.

Trip Trap represents a playful departure from the despairing underpinnings of Kerouac's preoccupations. But in most writings after *The Dharma Bums,* Kerouac continues the spiritual journey, retelling his trip of isolation to Desolation Peak, testing the teachings of Snyder and the "Zen lunatics." Stylistically, the prose structures of the first section of *Desolation Angels* (written in 1956, published in 1965) have bridges that join one block of writing to the next, like jazz riffs, but they are also experiments in small form, as in: "Desolation, Desolation,/ so hard/ To come down off of." This bridge illustrates another of Kerouac's uses for haiku. He appropriates the form and modifies it, so that the awkward third line, "To come down off of," reads with difficulty, its preposition at end mirroring the poet's arduous descent.

Strict critics doubt whether these are haiku at all. Because Kerouac makes distinctions among the various short poems in his canon, one might well question these departures from the strict Japanese models he so admired.[11] While Kerouac was well versed in the haiku books of his time, and a diligent, disciplined practitioner of the genre, he also felt free, exercising a kind of poetic license in their experimental use.

---

11. In addition to reading Blyth's translations in its four volumes, Kerouac owned several collections: *Japanese Haiku: Two Hundred Twenty Examples of Seventeen-Syllable Poems by Bashō, Buson, Issa, Shiki, Sokan, Kikaku Chiyo-Ni, Joso, Yaha Boncho, and Others* (Mount Vernon: The Peter Pauper Press, 1955, 1956) and *An Introduction to Haiku: An Anthology of Poems and Poets from Bashō to Shiki,* with translations and commentary by Harold G. Henderson (Garden City: Doubleday Anchor Original, 1958). By 1964, he was lamenting the loss of one of his Blyth books and "my only copy of Zoot Sims-Al Cohn-me haikus album" (pocket notebook #43).

Haiku Genre

Contemporary poets such as Cor van den Heuvel became interested in haiku after reading *The Dharma Bums*. A flourishing American haiku tradition is much admired by poets worldwide,[12] and many cite Kerouac's efforts as an early influence. Nevertheless, a great deal of wrangling takes place among haiku poets today over formal distinctions that I suspect Kerouac would have disdained. While many contemporary haiku poets acknowledge Kerouac as an influence, their work does not build off his, but goes in another direction, more closely aligned to the Japanese sources. As to Kerouac, they ponder, did he write haiku at all, or perhaps senryu?

---

12. When asked what he considered to be the current state of poetry in 1993, Nobel Prize–winning poet Czeslaw Milosz replied, "I take interest . . . in the American haiku movement. . . . For me this is a very interesting trend." Quoted by Thomas Lynch in "A Way of Awareness: The Emerging Delineaments of American Haiku" (unpublished essay).

I Introduction I

Haiku's sister genre, senryu, is defined as following the same form as haiku, but where the latter deals with Nature, senryu is specifically about human nature and human relationships and is often humorous. Technically, haiku contains a seasonal reference; senryu does not. Unlike the more demanding haiku, senryu can employ what Kerouac saw as "poetic trickery": simile, metaphor, and personification. That Kerouac often wrote his haiku indenting at the second line, as Blyth did for senryu, indicates his understanding of the distinction.

Haiku poet Alan Pizzarelli finds that Kerouac mastered (knowingly or not) not only haiku, but its related forms— short tanka (equivalent to a Western sonnet), haibun or prose written by a haiku poet (in *Desolation Angels* and *Big Sur*), and renku, the kind of linked poetry that characterized the haiku in *Some of the Dharma*.[13]

Whether he was aware or not, Kerouac both managed a full range of variants and attempted to stay within the scope of haiku standards. His instincts were sufficiently attuned to

13. Pizzarelli, "Modern Senryu," (unpublished essay).

the haiku spirit in whatever genre; many of his poems are haiku or senryu parodies: "How that butterfly'll wake up" (1957) plays off Buson's "On the hanging bell/Has perched and is fast asleep,/A butterfly!" Similarly, "Runover by my lawn-mower" is a comic response to Bashō's classic "The old pond, yes!/—the water jumped into/By a frog"—(Kerouac's translit-eration, 1959).

While Kerouac understood the discipline of haiku, often his attempts are more playful than rigorous:

In my medicine cabinet   The summer chair
    the winter fly   rocking by itself
Has died of old age   In the blizzard

Each poem reveals the essence of haiku through simplicity of expression and compression. That the "winter" fly has died of old age implies that we are in a season past winter, spring per-haps, or summer. So the use of winter is a play on the traditional seasonal reference. The winter fly's plight suggests human mor-tality as well, moving toward the "winter," or old age. In "The summer chair," the seasonal reference comes as a surprise at the poem's third line; the scene depicts winter, the inanimate chair is enlivened but, like man, subject to the vagaries of Nature.

Kerouac revised other poems in an attempt to wrestle with the implications of the seasonal reference. For example, he selected the following poem for his Book of Haikus:

Straining at the padlock,
    the garage doors
At noon

An earlier version found in the notebooks includes the seasonal reference, the last line reading: "At noon in May." Pizzarelli has suggested that the noon heat implies that it is summer. No need to mention the season, as in traditional haiku, and thereby add syllables. That Kerouac selected the shorter version for his Book of Haikus demonstrates he revised his poems in order to achieve greater concision. On the other hand, Kerouac also occasionally played with the seasonal reference to make a nonhaiku evocation haiku-ish: as in "Mao Tse Tung has taken/too many Siberian sacred/Mushrooms in Autumn."

Pops

In the chair
    I decided to call Haiku
By the name of Pop

Kerouac's decision to call haiku by the name of "pops" may also announce his departure from haiku tradition. As his notebooks show, this vacillation between embracing and rejecting the traditions of haiku continued throughout his career, through a variety of stages: the first is his 1956 Desolation period, when he completed *Some of the Dharma,* "Desolation Pops," and *Desolation Angels.* In this phase, which was laden with references to Zen Buddhism, Kerouac saw an opportunity to utilize the Japanese form to evoke his larger concerns, intoning the Void and other abstractions as an attempt to grapple with and describe mystical experience. Renaming them signals the veering off from a classical approach: "Time keeps running out/—sweat/On my brow, from playing." The construction is complicated and confusing, as if Kerouac were oblivious to standard haiku strategies of using the present tense and concrete images; he loses the succinct image haiku is so well suited to achieve. And yet, the juxtaposition of the first part with the second underscores Kerouac's points about eternity and the ongoing nature of the universe. While this writing does not exemplify haiku ideals, nevertheless, it partakes in a sweeping surreal image characteristic of Kerouac's writing at large.

As in his prose works, Kerouac's poetry reveals a similar pattern of development: from the conventional to the experimental. Never a formalist, he wrote many experimental haiku. Some he merely tossed off, and came back to, refining as he went along. As the poems contained in *Some of the Dharma* and his notebooks show, Kerouac considered haiku a loose designation, a springboard to dive from, one he could use freely for his own artistic ends.[14]

---

14. This idea of Kerouac's use of haiku beyond the production of poetry adds a dimension to the prevailing and merely biographical

Beat Generation Haiku

Fall trees—
    dog knocks—
Old Itch   (a Beat generation haiku)

An original scroll manuscript, entitled "Is there a Beat Generation?" had this haiku embedded within it, including the parenthetical epithet. Kerouac's essay rants against the term "beat generation" being used out of hand. The haiku is a

---

one put forth by Barbara Ungar: "His Buddhism was largely an attempt to come to peace with the life described in his prose: his haiku express his attempts to transcend it." Going on, Ungar finds that "[h]is haiku describe the rare moments when Kerouac found inner peace, when he stopped running long enough to look and feel deeply the nature of this tragic, fleeting world. But his peace never lasted, his enlightenment never came, and haiku remained a secondary art form to him." (Ungar, "Jack Kerouac as Haiku Poet," in *Haiku in English,* Stanford Honors Essays in Humanities 21, Stanford, 1978.)

spontaneous expression of his irritation with the use of the term by those who have no place using it. "Woe" to them, he wrote. Yet this three-liner, perhaps more evocative of Kerouac's emotional state than of the world outside, provides a category of its own and represents another stage in his appropriation of haiku. Kerouac also wrote many two-line haiku, here and in his notebooks. Many haiku poets today utilize the two-line form. This poem appears nowhere else in Kerouac's published work, nor in the notebooks. But it is found in an essay entitled "The Beat Generation," along with other haiku so labeled.[15] Should we regard it as haiku at all, even if he does? Does it refer to another, more successful haiku?

The tree
    looks like a dog,
Barking at heaven

---

15. Rare Books and Manuscripts Library at Columbia University. The essay is typed out, as are many scruffy "haikus," under the beat generation banner, some as two-line haiku.

This poem, from a pocket notebook, conveys Kerouac's anger and frustration in a universal vision, personifying nature in contempt of a bewildering and indifferent "heaven." Significantly, Kerouac selected it for his Book of Haikus. Written in Northport, in the fall of 1958, it coincides in composition with the "beat generation haiku," where he eschews the deliberate haiku form to create the more surreal juxtapositions that mark his more experimental prose.

————

What follows here should give a range of Kerouac's haiku production. Just as he will remain controversial as a prose stylist, so too will his work be reevaluated and be controversial for critics of haiku. He will continue to be thought a pioneer, as someone who opened up the genre. This collection should counter the prevailing assumption that for Jack Kerouac, haiku was merely a secondary art. Quite to the contrary, as he wrote to his Italian translator, Fernanda Pivano, in April of 1964, "The large body of sustained work that I have created, all of that [is] poetry turned into narrative drama. . . ." Even in this tight poetic expression, he will always be revered as a daring literary artist.

REGINA WEINREICH
June 2002

Acknowledgments

In April 1997, at Allen Ginsberg's memorial service held in a Buddhist meditation center, John Sampas, executor of Jack Kerouac's estate, asked if I might put together a volume of haiku. I am deeply grateful to him for entrusting this important work to me. Further thanks are owed to my editor Paul Slovak, wise to books and beats, and to the literary agents Jennifer Lyons and Sterling Lord. Additional suggestions came from Gary Snyder, David Stanford, Hiroaki Sato, Ann Charters, Bertrand Agostini, Joyce Johnson, Douglas Brinkley, and James Hackett, who lives in Haiku, Hawaii. Philip Whalen was already too ill to correspond with me: I am grateful for his good faith. Stanley Twardowicz of Northport shared poetry and anecdotes about Jack writing them. The librarians and staff at the Berg Collection of the New York Public Library and Rare Books and Manuscripts Room at Columbia University's Butler Library deserve special recognition.

I have been guided by modern haiku poets. Especially generous with his time and good advice has been Cor van den Heuvel who brought me an indispensable first edition of

Acknowledgments

Blyth's four-volume *Haiku*. Lee Gurga and Alan Pizzarelli, too, helped hone my haiku aesthetics. As to selection, these poets advised me, best to throw away the clinkers. Even a superb haiku poet will write hundreds before a single good one surfaces. Best not to show Kerouac at his worst.

Ultimately I have chosen many against their sound counsel. As part of Kerouac's grand design, his "Divine Comedy of the Buddha," Kerouac's haiku are an invaluable record of his language. Readers deserve to see them and like them as they will. Let us say I have erred on the side of extravagance.

A rare moment — Neighbor
boy in quiet moonlight
Looking thru telescope

(And doesn't know I'm there
in next yard)

(And moon so silent
& clean)

(Oh how to compare all
that in a NINE-WORD
AMERICAN HAIKUS)
↓

How rare! — quiet
moonlit night boy
Gazing thru telescope

(Get rid of articles &
prepositions) ?

RARE WORLD MOMENT
— MOONLIGHT TELESCOPE BOY
STUDYING QUIET MOON

—I—

Book of Haikus

"Book of Haikus not collected yet but my latest
haiku the best:

> Chief Crazy Horse looks
> North with tearful eyes—
> The first snow flurry

. . . would collect all my haikus from notebooks
and put together for a book . . ."

Letters to Lawrence Ferlinghetti
October 23, November 1961

Jack Kerouac's selections of haiku for publication were placed in a black folder marked "Book of Haikus." Most originate in the pocket notebooks starting in 1956. While no date is given for the contents of this folder, it is clear from journals and letters that Kerouac meant to publish them. In *Some of the Dharma*, he listed his intended books, including a Book of Haikus. "American Haikus," recorded in 1959 with Al Cohn and Zoot Sims, were taken from this collection, as were most in the selection known as *Scattered Poems*.

Book of Haikus

The little sparrow
   on my eave drainpipe
Is looking around

                    The tree looks
                       like a dog
                    Barking at Heaven

Girl with wagon—
what do
I know?

Tuesday—one more
drop of rain
From my roof

I found my
cat—one
Silent star

In the morning frost
the cats
Stepped slowly

No telegram today
　　—Only more
Leaves fell

　　　　　Frozen
　　　　　　in the birdbath,
　　　　A leaf

First December cold
　　wave—not even
One cricket

　　　　　Cool breeze—maybe
　　　　　　just a shillyshallying show
　　　　That'll ruin everything

50 miles from N.Y.
    all alone in Nature,
The squirrel eating

                    2 traveling salesmen
                        passing each other
                    On a Western road

The smoke of old
    naval battles
Is gone

                    The windmills of
                        Oklahoma look
                    In every direction

6

Grain elevators, waiting
      for the road
To approach them

                    Juju beads on
                        Zen manual—
                    My knees are cold

Listen to the birds sing!
      All the little birds
Will die!

                    Dusk—the bird
                        on the fence
                    A contemporary of mine

7

Nightfall—too dark
  to read the page,
Too cold

Useless! useless!
  —heavy rain driving
Into the sea

Alone at home reading
  Yoka Daishi,
Drinking tea

The bottoms of my shoes
  are clean
From walking in the rain

Coming from the west,
    covering the moon,
Clouds—not a sound

        Her yellow dolls bowing
            on the shelf—
        My dead step grandmother

Birds singing
 in the dark
In the rainy dawn

        Straining at the padlock,
            the garage doors
        At noon

Nodding against the wall,
  the flowers
Sneeze

The earth winked
   at me—right
In the john

November the seventh
   The last
Faint cricket

Well here I am,
   2 PM—
What day is it?

Nodding against the wall,
 The flowers
Sneeze

That's an unencouraging sign,
 The fish store
Is closed   ← (dream)

The strumming of the trees
 harkenes me back
To immortal afternoon

Reading concluding parts of SWANN'S WAY
with utter amazement, the reappearance
of Swann as Gilberte's father in a
grey hat and hood in Champs-Elysees on
a winter afternoon, Ah, it's as tho I'd
lived it myself & written it —— I tell
you I had an eerie sensation in Paris, of
having lived there before, suffered terribly there
it was too familiar and painful——
  Well now for the trilogy
    BOY, YOUNG WRITER, BUDDHIST
BOY — 1922-1938
Y.W. — 1938-1953
BU'ST — 1953-1960
  The finale will be HERMIT (1960—?)
A pinch of the Monad oughta translate me
into the pure serene eastern Connichar ——
that's how the fat grass grows

In my medicine cabinet
    the winter fly
Has died of old age

                    The castle of the Gandharvas
                        is full of aging
                    Young couples

Early morning yellow flowers
    —Thinking about
The drunkards of Mexico

                    Wine at dawn
                        —The long
                    Rainy sleep

Night fall—too dark
    to read the page,
Too dark

                        What is Buddhism?
                            —A crazy little
                        Bird blub

Crossing the football field,
    coming home from work,
The lonely businessman

                        Prayerbeads
                            on the Holy Book
                        —My knees are cold

After the shower,
    among the drenched roses,
The bird thrashing in the bath

                    The barn, swimming
                        in a sea
                    Of windblown leaves

The low yellow
    moon above
The quiet lamplit house

                    Snap yr finger,
                        stop the world!
                    —Rain falls harder

Beautiful young girls running
  up the library steps
With shorts on

                              Bee, why are you
                                staring at me?
                              I'm not a flower!

Nored the Atlantican Astrologer
  weeps because the King
Laid his Autumn girl

                              Ghengis Khan looks fiercely
                                east, with red eyes,
                              Hungering for Autumn vengeance

Geronimo, in Autumn
	says no to peaceful
Cochise—Smoke rises

				Mao Tse Tung has taken
					too many Siberian sacred
				Mushrooms in Autumn

Quiet moonlit night—
	Neighbor boy studying
By telescope;—"Ooo!"

				Missing a kick
					at the icebox door
				It closed anyway

Perfect moonlit night
   marred
By family squabbles

                    The Spring moon—
                       How many miles away
                    Those orange blossoms!

When the moon sinks
   down to the power line,
I'll go in

                    Looking up at the stars,
                       feeling sad,
                    Going "tsk tsk tsk"

This July evening,
    A large frog
On my doorsill

                    Dawn, a falling star
                        —A dewdrop lands
                    On my head!

In back of the Supermarket,
  in the parking lot weeds,
Purple flowers

                    Protected by the clouds,
                        the moon
                    Sleeps sailing

Chief Crazy Horse
  looks tearfully north
The first snow flurries

November—how nasal
  the drunken
Conductor's call

In Autumn Geronimo
  weeps—no pony
With a blanket

Autumn night in New Haven
  —the Whippenpoofers
Singing on the train

Peeking at the moon
  in January, Bodhisattva
Takes a secret piss

               A turtle sailing along
                 on a log,
               Head up

A black bull
  and a white bird
Standing together on the shore

               Catfish fighting for his life,
                 and winning,
               Splashing us all

The poppies!—
  I could die
In delicacy now

            Summer night—
              the kitten playing
            With the Zen calendar

Trying to study sutras,
  the kitten on my page
Demanding affection

            Hurrying things along,
              Autumn rain
            On my awning

All the wash
  on the line
Advanced one foot

                        That's an unencouraging sign,
                          the fish store
                        is closed

A whole pussywillow
  over there,
Unblown

                        The moon is white—
                          the lamps are
                        Yellow

Listening to birds using
   different voices, losing
My perspective of History

                    The crickets—crying
                       for rain—
                    Again?

Gray orb of the moon
  behind silver clouds—
The Spanish moss

                    Dawn wind
                       in the spruces
                    —The late moon

Twilight—the bird
    in the bush
In the rain

                    Ignoring my bread,
                        the bird peeking
                    In the grass

Spring night—
    a leaf falling
From my chimney

                    My cat eating
                        at his saucer
                    —Spring moon

Rainy night
   —I put on
My pajamas

                 Black bird—no!
                    bluebird—pear
                 Branch still jumping

Wash hung out
   by moonlight
—Friday night

                 The postman is late
                    —The toilet window
                 Is shining

Dusk—boy
  smashing dandelions
With a stick

            Holding up my purring
              cat to the moon,
            I sighed

All day long wearing
  a hat that wasn't
On my head

            The national scene
              —late afternoon sun
            In those trees

Glow worm sleeping
   on this flower,
Your light's on!

                August moon—oh
                   I got a boil
                On my thigh

Empty baseball field
   —A robin,
Hops along the bench

                Following each other,
                   my cats stop
                When it thunders

My rumpled couch
　　—The lady's voice
Next door

Spring evening—
　　the two
Eighteen year old sisters

Drunk as a hoot owl
　　writing letters
By thunderstorm

Brighter than the night,
　　my barn roof
Of snow

Gray spring rain
    —I never clipped
My hedges

                              The rain has filled
                                   the birdbath
                              Again, almost

My rose arbor knows more
  about June
Than it'll know about winter

                              Late moon rising
                                   —Frost
                              On the grass

The beautiful red
  dogwood tree
Waiting for the cross

                          Bird bath thrashing,
                            by itself—
                          Autumn wind

A mother & son
  just took a shortcut
Thru my yard

                          Beautiful summer night
                            gorgeous as the robes
                          Of Jesus

Eleven quick skulks
    to Fall
And still cool

                    Woke up groaning
                        with a dream of a priest
                    Eating chicken necks

And the quiet cat
    sitting by the post
Perceives the moon

                    Ancient ancient world
                        —tight skirts
                    By the new car

Waiting for the leaves
   to fall;—
There goes one!

                              First frost dropped
                                 all leaves
                              Last night—leafsmoke

Evening coming—
   The office girl
unloosing her scarf

                              The housecats, amazed
                                 at something new,
                              Looking in the same direction

32

The word HANDICAPPED
  sliding over snow
On a newspaper

                              Run over by my lawnmower,
                                 waiting for me to leave,
                              The frog

A raindrop from
  the roof
Fell in my beer

                              A bird on
                                 the branch out there
                              —I waved

Cat eating fish heads
  —All those eyes
In the starlight

                    The moon had
                      a cat's mustache,
                    For a second

Seven birds in a tree,
  looking
In every direction

                    The birds
                      surprise me
                    On all sides

Cat gone 24 hours
   —A piece of his hair
Waving on the door

                         How flowers love
                            the sun,
                         Blinking there!

Asking Albert Saijo
 for a haiku,
He said nothing

                         In a Mojave dust storm
                            Albert said: "Senzeie,
                         Was a Mongolian waif"

The summer chair
  rocking by itself
In the blizzard

              My pipe unlit
                beside the Diamond
              Sutra—What to think?

February gales—racing
  westward through
The clouds, the moon

              Among the nervous birds
                the mourning dove
              Nibbles quietly

Cold gray tufts
   of winter grass
Under the stars

                    Memère says: "Planets are
                       far apart so people
                    Can't bother each other."

In the quiet house,
   my mother's
Moaning yawns

                    Blizzard in the suburbs
                       —the mailman
                    And the poet walking

Blizzard in the suburbs
   —old men driving slowly
To the store 3 blocks

Dusk—The blizzard
  hides everything,
Even the night

A full November moon
 and mild,
Mary Carney

Mild spring night—
  a teenage girl said
"Good evening" in the dark

Spring night—the sound
 of the cat
Chewing fish heads

I said a joke
        under the stars
        —No laughter

(Tonight) that star
     is waving & flaming
Something awful

Perfectly silent
        in the starry night,
The little tree

White rose with red
  splashes—Oh
Vanilla ice cream cherry!

                    Looking for my cat
                        in the weeds,
                    I found a butterfly

Churchbells ringing in town
    —The caterpillar
In the grass

                    For a moment
                        the moon
                    Wore goggles

Iowa clouds
    following each other
Into Eternity

The sleeping moth—
        he doesn't know
The lamps turned up again

Reading my notes—
    The fly stepping from
The page to the finger

August in Salinas—
        Autumn leaves in
Clothing store displays

Autumn night
    low moon—
Fire in Smithtown

Full moon of October
    —The tiny mew
of the Kitty

Cool sunny autumn day,
    I'll mow the lawn
one last time

A yellow witch chewing
    a cigarette,
Those Autumn leaves

I've turned up
 the lamp again
—The sleeping moth

Train tunnel, too dark
 for me to write: that
"Men are ignorant"

The flies on the porch
 and the fog on the peaks
Are so sad

The cow, taking a big
 dreamy crap, turning
To look at me

Leaves skittering on
   the tin roof
—August fog in Big Sur

                    Terraces of fern
                       in the dripping
                    Redwood shade

Here comes the nightly
   moth, to his nightly
Death, at my lamp

                    Halloween colors
                       orange and black
                    On a summer butterfly

Fighting over a peach
    stone, bluejays
In the bushes

                        Barefoot by the sea,
                            stopping to scratch one ankle
                        With one toe

Summer afternoon—
    impatiently chewing
The jasmine leaf

                        Giving an apple
                            to the mule, the big lips
                        Taking hold

Bluejay drinking at my
    saucer of milk,
Throwing his head back

The mule, turning
    slowly, rubbing his
Behind on a log

Nibbling his ankle,
    the mule's teeth
Like kettle drum

Front hooves spread,
    the mule scratches his
Neck along a log

46

A quiet moment—
    low lamp, low logs—
Just cooking the stew

                              One foot on the bar
                                  of soap,
                              The Bluejay peeking

Quietly pouring coffee
  in the afternoon,
How pleasant!

                              Bird suddenly quiet
                                  on his branch—his
                              Wife glancing at him

47

Four bluejays quiet
  in the afternoon tree,
Occasionally scratching

                    The hermit's broom,
                      the fire, the kettle
                    —August night

The cricket in my cellar window, this quiet
    Sunday afternoon

                    As the cool evenings
                      make them selves felt,
                    Smoke from suburban chimneys

48

Cold crisp October morning
 —the cats fighting
In the weeds

Drunken deterioration—
     ho-hum,
Shooting star

This October evening,
   the velvet eyes
Of Manjuri

Washing my face
   with snow
Beneath the Little Dipper

A balloon caught
    in the tree—dusk
In Central Park zoo

                  Elephants munching
                     on grass—loving
                  Heads side by side

The stars are racing
    real fast
Through the clouds

                  Dawn—crows cawing,
                    ducks quack quacking,
                  Kitchen windows lighting

Breakfast done
  the tomcat curls up
On the down couch

                        Dawn—the writer who
                              hasn't shaved,
                        Poring over notebooks

February dawn—frost
  on the path
Where I paced all winter

                        Blizzard's just started
                              all that bread scattered,
                        And just one bird

The trees, already
  bent in the windless
Oklahoma plain

                    In the desert sun
                      in Arizona,
                    A yellow railroad caboose

The new moon
  is the toe nail
Of God

                    Sunny day—bird tracks
                      & cat tracks
                    In the snow

Little pieces of ice
   in the moonlight
Snow, thousands of em

                      The cat: a little
                          body being used
                      By a little person

Perfect circle round
 the moon
In the center of the sky

                      Standing on the end
                        on top of the tree,
                      The Big Dipper

Who wd have guessed
   that a January moon
Could be so orange!

                              A big fat flake
                               of snow
                              Falling all alone

Dawn—the tomcat
   hurrying home
With his tail down

                              Buddhas in moonlight
                                —Mosquito bite
                              Thru hole in my shirt

54

After supper
    on crossed paws,
The cat meditates

                    Closing the book,
                        rubbing my eyes—
                    The sleepy August dawn

Resting watchfully, the cat
    and the squirrel
Share the afternoon

                    The gently moving
                        leaves
                    Of the August afternoon

A long island
    in the sky
The Milky Way

                        Haunted Autumn visiting
                          familiar August,
                        These last 2 days

Disturbing my mind essence,
    all that food
I have to cook

                        Arms folded
                          to the moon,
                        Among the cows

Birds flying north—
    Where are the squirrels?—
There goes a plane to Boston

        So humid you cant
           light matches, like
        Living in a tank

Barley soup in Scotland
  in November—
Misery everywhere

Dharma Pops

Dharma—Notes in any form about the Dharma.
BOOK OF DHARMAS

All takes place in present tense

POP—American (non-Japanese) Haikus, short
3-line poems or "pomes" rhyming or non-rhyming
delineating "little Samadhis" if possible, usually of
a Buddhist connotation, aiming towards enlighten-
ment. BOOK OF POPS.

(Some of the Dharma)

Using Kerouac's definition of Dharma as the Law of Things, the True Law, the Verity, the Dharma Pops are haiku in action, as they appear in several books: *Some of the Dharma* (1953–1956), *Maggie Cassidy* (1953), "Lucien Midnight/Old Angel Midnight" (1957), *Lonesome Traveler* (1960), *Heaven & Other Poems* (1959), *Trip Trap: Haiku along the Road from San Francisco to New York* (1959), *Pomes All Sizes* (1955–1960), and *Scattered Poems* (1945–1969).

Mad wrote curtains
        of
poetry on fire
            October 28, 1954

Dharma Pops

FROM *SOME OF THE DHARMA*
(1953–1956)
Change Su Chi's art
    studio, a silent
Shade in the window

                        The sun keeps getting
                            dimmer—foghorns
                        began to blow in the bay

Time keeps running out
      —sweat
On my brow, from playing

                        The sky is still empty,
                              The rose is still
                        On the typewriter keys

Rain's over, hammer on wood
      —this cobweb
Rides the sun shine

                        In the sun
                              the butterfly wings
                        Like a church window

In the chair
    I decided to call Haiku
By the name of Pop

                    The purple wee flower
                        should be reflected
                    In that low water

The red roof of the barn
    is ravelled
Like familiar meat

                    Swinging on delicate hinges
                        the Autumn Leaf
                    Almost off the stem

Rainy night,
   the top leaves wave
In the gray sky

THE LIGHT BULB
   SUDDENLY WENT OUT—
STOPPED READING.

Taghagata neither loathes
   nor loves
His body's milk or shit

Looking around to think
   I saw the thick white cloud
Above the house

Looking up to see
    the airplane
I only saw the TV aerial

                              My butterfly came
                                  to sit in my flower,
                              Sir Me

You'd be surprised
    how little I knew
Even up to yesterday

                              Two Japanese boys
                                  singing
                              Inky Dinky Parly Voo

Take up a cup of water
    from the ocean
And there I am

                        Leaf dropping straight
                            In the windless midnight:
                        The dream of change

Stop slipping me
    Your old Diamond Sutra
You illimitable tight-ass!

                        Or, walking the same or different
                            paths
                        The moon follows each

Old man dying in a room—
    Groan
At five o'clock

                    The mist in front
                        of the morning mountains
                    —late Autumn

Samsara in the morning
    —puppy yipping,
Hot motor steaming

                    Praying all the time—
                        talking
                    To myself

The Sunny Breeze
    will come to me
Presently

                            Coming from the West,
                                covering the moon,
                            Clouds—not a sound

Phantom Rose
    Lust
Is a Leopard

                            I drink my tea
                                and say
                            Hm hm

Dusk in the holy
    woods—
Dust on my window

                The bird came on the branch
                    —danced three times—
                And burred away

The raindrops have plenty
    of personality—
Each one

                Me, you—you, me
                    Everybody—
                He-he

Do you know why my name is Jack?
    Why?
That's why.

                              Wild to sit on a haypile,
                                  Writing Haikus,
                              Drinkin wine

Waitin for the Zipper
    4 PM—
Sun in West clouds, gold

                              Gull sailing
                                  in the saffron sky—
                              The Holy Ghost wanted it

Water in a hole
   —behold
The sodden skies

                    Rain in North Carolina
                       —the saints
                    Are still meditating

The yellow dolls bow—
   Poor lady
Is dead

                    Haiku, shmaiku, I cant
                       understand the intention
                    Of reality

I went in the woods
  to meditate—
It was too cold

Early morning with the
  happy dogs—
I forgot the Path

What could be newer? this
  new little bird
Not yet summer fat!

The dog yawned
  and almost swallowed
My Dharma

Concatenation!—the bicycle
    pulls the wagon
Because the rope is tied

                        White clouds of this steamy planet
                            obstruct
                        My vision of the blue void

Grass waves,
    hens chuckle,
Nothing's happening

                        A spring mosquito
                            dont even know
                        How to bite!

All that ocean of blue
   soon as those clouds
Pass away

                Propped up on my shoe
                  the Diamond Sutra—
                Propped up on a pine root

Silent pipe—
   peace and quiet
In my heart

                Why'd I open my eyes?
                  because
                I wanted to

There is no deep
    turning-about
In the Void

                    The pine woods
                        move
                    In the mist

There's no Buddha
    because
There's no me

                    Emptiness
                        of the Ananda glass bead,
                    Is the bowing weeds

WARM WIND
  makes the pines
Talk Deep

Spring dusk
  on Fifth Avenue,
A bird

Gary (Snyder) gone from the shack
  like smoke
—My lonely shoes

Two ants hurry
  to catch up
With lonely Joe

Hummingbird hums
 hello—bugs
Race and swoop

                        Morning sun—
                            The purple petals,
                        Four have fallen

FROM *LONESOME TRAVELER*
(1960, FROM 1957 NOTEBOOK)
Walking along the night beach,
 —Military music
On the boulevard.

                        FROM *HEAVEN & OTHER POEMS*
                        (1959)
                        The little worm
                         lowers itself from the roof
                        By a self shat thread

Grain Elevators are tall trucks
   that let the road
approach them

          Grain Elevators on
             Saturday waiting for
        The farmers to come home

Shall I say no?
   —fly rubbing
its back legs

          The moon,
             the falling star
         —Look elsewhere

FROM *POMES ALL SIZES* (1955–1960, PUBLISHED 1992)

Came down from my

   ivory tower

And found no world

—III—

1956
Desolation Pops

SPRING

Gary Snyder's Haiku (Spoken on the Mountain)

"Talking about the literary
life—the yellow
aspens."

It is raining—
I guess I'll make
Some tea (Your haiku)

(Letter to Gary Snyder)

On June 18, 1956, perhaps replicating the experience of Han Shan, the Chinese poet to whom *The Dharma Bums* was dedicated, Kerouac isolated himself on Desolation Peak. For sixty-three days he reflected on nature and wrote in the spirit of Zen Buddhism. These haiku experiments—often prosaic and Western like his "Dharma Pops"—represent Kerouac's efforts in relating his mountain loneliness to Nature and mystical experience: The "Desolation Pops" manuscript is a collection of seventy-two, numbered by the author, typed up; many originate in pocket notebook #1, "Desolation Peak"; a selection from *Desolation Angels* (Part I, 1956) and 1956 notebooks and letters are also included here.

Desolation Pops

(**NOTE:** <u>Desolation</u> is the name of the mountain . . .
<u>Pops</u> are American free-syllabled haikus . . .)

(1)
Morning meadow—
  Catching my eye,
One weed

(2)
Poor tortured teeth
  under
The blue sky

(3)

Ate a Coney Island
  hamburger
In Vancouver Washington

(4)

Run after that
  body—run after
A raging fire

(5)

Work of the quiet
  mountain, this
Torrent of purity

(6)

Sun on the rocks—
  a fighting snag
Holds on

(7)

A stump with sawdust
  —a place
To meditate

(8)

The smiling fish—
  where are they,
Scouting bird?

(9)

Me, my pipe,
　my folded legs—
Far from Buddha

(10)

I close my eyes—
　I hear & see
Mandala

(11)

The clouds assume
　as I assume,
Faces of hermits

(12)

Satisfied, the pine
　bough washing
In the waters

(13)

Content, the top trees
　shrouded
In gray fog

(14)

Bred to rejoice,
　the giggling
Sunshine leaves

(15)

Cradled and warm,
  the upper snow,
The trackless

(16)

Everlastingly loose
  and responsive,
The cloud business

(17)

Everywhere beyond
  the Truth,
Empty space blue

(18)

The mountains
  are mighty patient,
Buddha-man

(19)

Ship paint
  on
An old T-shirt

(20)

Snow melting,
  streams rushing—
Lookouts leave the valley

(21)
Man—nothing but
  a
Rain barrel

(22)
Debris on the lake
  —my soul
Is upset

(23)
Gee last night—
  dreamed
Of Harry Truman

(24)
There's nothing there
  because
I dont care

(25)
In the late afternoon
  peaks, I see
The hope

(26)
The top of Jack
  Mountain—done in
By golden clouds

(27)

Hmf—Ole Starvation Ridge
   is
Milkied o'er

(28)

All the insects ceased
   in honor
Of the moon

(29)

The taste
   of rain—
Why kneel?

(30)

Full moon, white snow,—
   my bottle
Of purple jello

(31)

I'm so mad
   I could bite
The mountaintops

(32)

Hot coffee
   and a cigarette—
why zazen?

(33)

Aurora Borealis
  over Hozomeen—
The void is stiller

(34)

Nat Wills, a tramp
  —America
In 1905

(35)

I'm back here in the middle
  of nowhere—
At least I think so

(36)

Poor gentle flesh—
  there is
No answer

(37)

The storm,
  like Dostoevsky
Builds up as it lists

(38)

What is a rainbow,
  Lord?—a hoop
For the lowly

(39)
Get to go—
  fork a hoss
And head for Mexico

(42)
Wednesday blah
  blah blah—
My mind hurts

(40)
Late afternoon—
  the mop is drying
On the rock

(43)
Kicked the cupboard
  and hurt my toe
—Rage

(41)
Late afternoon—
  my bare back's
Cold

(44)
Late afternoon—
  it's not the void
That changed

(45)
Sex—shaking to breed
　as
Providence permits

(48)
Thunder and snow—
　how
We shall go!

(46)
M'ugly spine—the loss
　of the kingdom
Of Heaven

(49)
The days go—
　They cant stay—
I don't realize

(47)
Thunder in the mountains—
　the iron
Of my mother's love

(50)
The creamer gives,
　the groaner quakes—
the angel smiles

(51)

A million acres
  of Bo-trees
And not one Buddha

(52)

Oh moon,
  such dismay?
—Earths betray

(53)

Skhandas my ass!
  —it's not
Even that

(54)

The moon
  is a
Blind lemon

(55)

Rig rig rig—
  that's the rat
On the roof

(56)

Made hot cocoa
  at night,
Sang by woodfire

(57)

I called Hanshan
  in the mountains
—there was no answer

(58)

What passes through
  is amusing
Himself being dew

(59)

I called Hanshan
  in the fog—
Silence, it said

(60)

I called—Dipankara
  instructed me
By saying nothing

(61)

I rubbed my bearded
  cheek and looked in
The mirror—Ki!

(62)

Mists blew by, I
  Closed my eyes,—
Stove did the talking

(63)

"Woo!"—bird of perfect
   balance on the fir
Just moved his tail

(64)

Bird was gone
   and distance grew
Immensely white

(65)

Misurgirafical & plomlied
   —ding dang
The Buddha's gang

(66)

Your belly's too big
   for your
Little teeth

(67)

But the Lost Creek trail
   they dont believe
Is in existence any more

(68)

Blubbery dubbery
   the chipmunk's
In the grass

(69)

Big wall of clouds
   from the North
Coming in—brrrr!

(70)

Aurora borealis
   over Mount Hozomeen—
The world is eternal

(71)

Chipmunk went in
   —butterfly
Came out

(72)

Holy sleep
   —Hanshan
Was right

On Starvation Ridge
  little sticks
Are trying to grow

                              Hitch hiked a thousand
                                miles and brought
                              You wine

A bubble, a shadow—
  woop—
The lightning flash

                              Mist boiling from the
                                ridge—the mountains
                              Are clean

Mist before the peak
—the dream
Goes on

The sound of silence
is all the instruction
You'll get

Desolation, Desolation,
wherefore have you
Earned your name?

While meditating
I am Buddha—
Who else?

Desolation, Desolation,
 so hard
To come down off of

                         Mayonnaise—
                          mayonnaise comes in cans
                         Down the river

Girls' footprints
 in the sand
—Old mossy pile

                         Wooden house
                          raw gray—
                         Pink light in the window

Neons, Chinese restaurants
  coming on—
Girls come by shades

New aluminum
  grammar school
In old lamplight

Napoleon in bronze
  the burning Blakean
mountains

Velvet horses
  in the valley auction—
Woman sings

River wonderland—
  The emptiness
Of the golden eternity

                              No imaginary judgments
                                  of form,
                              The clouds

Butterfat soil
  of the valley—
Big black slugs

                              God's dream,
                                It's only
                              A dream

America: fishing licenses
 the license
To meditate

Reflected upsidedown
 in the sunset lake, pines,
Pointing to infinity

All I see is what
 I see—
Red fire sunset

She loves Lysander
 not Demetrius—
Who?—Hermia

I don't care
  what
thusness is

                    Alpine fir with
                      snowcap't background—
                    It doesn't matter

Late afternoon—
  the lakes sparkle
Blinds me

                    I made raspberry fruit jello
                      The color of rubies
                    In the setting sun

Ah who cares?
 I'll do what I want—
Roll another joint

                    Sixty sunsets have I seen
                        revolve on this perpendicular hill

Nirvana, as when the rain
    puts out a little fire

                    Sunday—
                        the sky is blue,
                    The flowers are red

The red paper
   waves for the breeze
—the breeze

                              Flowers
                                 aim crookedly
                              At the straight death

1957
Road Haikus

SUMMER

SF is the poetry of a New Holy Lunacy like that of
ancient times (Li Po, Han Shan, Tom O Bedlam, Kit
Smart, Blake) yet it also has that mental discipline
typified by the haiku (Bashō, Buson), that is, the
discipline of pointing out things directly, purely,
concretely, no abstractions or explanations, wham
wham the true blue song of man.

"The Origins of Joy in Poetry"

Here is a fertile group of haiku, many written when Kerouac lived in Philip Whalen's cabin in Berkeley from May 16 to June 11, 1957. Before September 5, when *On the Road* was famously hailed as "an authentic work of art" marking "an historic occasion" in *The New York Times*, and catapulting him into national recognition, Kerouac's pocket notebooks contain haiku entries written in New York City, Tangier, Aix-en-Provence, London, New York City again, Berkeley, Mexico, and Orlando. As the notebooks and letters of this period show, Kerouac exhorted himself to write haiku, mindful of the traditional methods.

Road Haikus

Moon behind
    Black clouds—
Silver seas

                    Coffee beans!
                        —Methinks I smell
                    The Canaries!

Highest perfect fool—
  the wisdom
Of the two-legged rat

                    Abbid abbayd ingrat
                      —Lighthouse
                    On the Azores

A bottle of wine,
  a bishop—
Everything is God

                    "You and me"
                     I sang
                    Looking at the cemetery

Shall I heed God's commandment?
  —wave breaking
On the rocks—

                        Shall I break God's commandment?
                          Little fly
                        Rubbing its back legs

Blowing in an afternoon wind,
  on a white fence,
A cobweb

                        Spring is coming
                          Yep, all that equipment
                        For sighs

The vigorous bell-ringing priest
  the catch in the harbor

                              Rock rosed—behind the Casbah
                                the sun has disappearing act

Three pencils arranged,
  Three minutes,
Sambaghakaya, Nirvanakaya, Dharmakaya

                              "The wind agrees with me
                                  not the sun"—
                              Washlines

110

The barking dog—
  Kill him
With a bicycle wheel

                    Man dying—
                      Harbor lights
                    On still water

The microscopic red bugs
  In the sea-side sand
Do they meet and greet?

                    Hand in hand in a red valley
                      with the universal schoolteacher—
                    the first morning

Old man of Aix
    white hair, beret—
Gone up the Cezanne street

                        Who cares about the pop-off trees
                            of Provence?—
                        A road's a road

Somebody rang my bell
    I said who?
O it doesn't worldly care

                        O Sebastian, where art thou?
                            Pa, watch over us!
                        Saints, thank you!

Lonesome blubbers
   grinding out the decades
With wet lips

                    Full moon in the trees
                         —across the street,
                    the jail

My friend standing
   in my bedroom—
The spring rain

                    Moth sleeping
                         on the newly plastered wall
                    —the spring rain

The jazz trombone,
    The moving curtain,
—Spring rain

                            Greyhound bus,
                                flowing all night,
                            Virginia

My flashlight,
    where I put it this afternoon
Twisted away in sleep

                            The book
                                stands all by itself
                            on the shelf

My hand,
    A thing with hairs,
rising and falling with my belly

                      Here comes
                       My dragon—
                      goodbye!

Loves his own belly
    The way I love my life,
The white cat

                      The little white cat
                       Walks in the grass
                      With his tail up in the air

The white cat
    Is green in the tree shade,
Like Gauguin's horse

The dregs of my coffee
        Glisten
In the morning light

Haiku! Haiku!
    Still wears a bandage
Over his injured eye!

How'd those guys
    get in here,
those two flies?

The backyard I tried to draw
   —It still looks
The same

                  The son who wants solitude,
                    Enveloped
                  In his room

All these sages
   Sleep
With their mouths open

                  I hate the ecstasy
                    Of that rose,
                  That hairy rose

May grass—
　　Nothing much
To do

　　　　　A pussywillow grew there
　　　　　　At the foot
　　　　　Of the breathless tree

The earth keeps turning
　like a dreary
Immortal

　　　　　Gary Snyder
　　　　　　is a haiku
　　　　　far away

On the sidewalk
   A dead baby bird
For the ants

        How that butterfly'll wake up
           When someone
        Bongs that bell!

Waving goodbye,
 the little girl,
Backing up

        Why explain?
           bear burdens
        In silence

The ant struggles escaping
    from the web—
The spider's non-comment

                    The mind of the flower
                        regards my mind
                    Externally

Buddha laughing
    on Mt. Lanka!
Like Jimmy Durante!

                    The flowers don't seem
                        to mind
                    the stupid May sunshine

The rose moves
    like a Reichian disciple
On its stem

                    Suddenly the official
                        goes cross eyed
                    And floats away

The strumming of the trees
    reminded me
Of immortal afternoon

                    Forever and forever
                        everything's alright—
                    midnight woods

Voices of critics
    in the theater lobby—
A moth on the carpet

                            Birds chirp
                                fog
                            Bugs the gate

My Japanese blinds
    are down—
I'm reading about Ethiopia

                            My Christ blinds
                                are down—
                            I'm reading about Virgin

122

Winking over his pipe
    the Buddha lumberman
Nowhere

                            The Golden Gate
                                creaks
                            With sunset rust

Smell of burning leaves,
    The quiet pool at evening
In August

                            April mist—
                                under the pine
                            At midnight

Drizzle—
  Midnight pine,
I sit dry

                    Wet fog
                      shining
                    In lamplit leaves

Spring day—
  in my mind
Nothing

                    Late April
                      dusk bluster—
                    Lions & lambs

The train speeding
   thru emptiness
—I was a trainman

                 The trees are putting on
                    Noh plays—
                 Booming, roaring

Train on the horizon—
   my window
rattles

                 Mist falling
                    —Purple flowers
                 Growing

— v —

1958–1959
Beat Generation Haikus

AUTUMN

"Beat Generation means a generation passed over
into eternity. . . . The last trembling of a leaf, at
being one with all time, a sudden brilliance of
redness in the fall.

. . . The beat generation knows all about
haikus. . . ."

"The Beat Generation" (1958)

During this period Kerouac was living in Orlando and Northport. By 1958, the term "beat generation," coined ten years before, had lost its meaning for Kerouac's coterie of writers and was used pejoratively by critics. Preparing for the publication of *The Dharma Bums*, Kerouac continued to write haiku, but he was also retreating into alcoholism. "The Beat Generation" collection, placed at the beginning of this section, marks his most angry, subjective work playing off the haiku genre.

Beat Generation Haikus

> Red light on pingpong—the fire engine screams
> On my hat/a big shit—the crow flies.
> Under my hat/a big shit—the crow flies.

The beat generation knows all about haikus and we're now going to present you with a few sample haikus,

Autumn nite—
Lucien's wife
Playing the guitar

Autumn nite—
the boys
playing haiku.

Autumn nite—
my mother cuts her throat

Autumn nite
—Lucien leans to Jack
on the couch.

Autumn nite—
my mother remembers
my birth.

                    Late autumn nite
                    the last faint cricket.

The little sparrow on the eave drainpipe
My heart flutters

                    These little gray sparrows on the roof
                    I'll shoot my editor.

I gotta make it in terms/that anyone can understand/
Did I tell ya about my nightmare?

Cloudy autumn nite
—cold water drips
in the sink.

                    Autumnal
                    Cowflops—
                    but a man must
                    make a living.

Autumnal cowflops—
    a man
Makes a living.

                    Walking down road with Allen—
                        Walking down the road in Autumn.

Walking down the road
    with Allen
—An old dream
    the same dream.

                        Autumn night stove
                        —I've never been
                        on a farm before.

Jack reads his book
aloud at nite
—the stars come out.

                        Brokenback goodshit
                        Heap bigshot
                        among the Birchtrees.

Walking down the road with dog
—a crushed leaf

Walking with the dog on the road
—a crooked leaf.

Walking down the road with Jack—
a crushed snake.

Walking down the road
with dog—
a crushed snake.

Walking down the road/a crushed snake.
autumn
Red trees—

                           Red trees—
                           the dog tears at
                           an old itch.

Fall trees
Dog knocks old itch

* * * * * * * * * * *

                           Puddles at dusk
                              —one drop
                         fell

Lilacs at dusk
     —one petal
fell

                    On Desolation
                     I was the alonest man
                    in the world

Moon in the
   bird bath—
One star too

                    I don't care—
                     the low yellow
                    Moon loves me

High noon
 in Northport
—Alien shore

The night
 is red
 with stars

Glow worms
 brightly sleeping
On my flowers

Wind too strong
 —empty nest
At midnight

My blue spruce
      in the pale
Haze dusk

                        August Moon Universe
                              —neither new
                        Nor old

The Angel's hair
      trailed on my chin
Like a cobweb

                        Stare intently
                              at my candle
                        —Pool of wax

September raindrops
    from my roof—
Soon icicles

                          Night rain—neighbors
                              Arguing loud voices
                          In next house

Four in morning—
    creak my mother
In her bed

                          Lay the pencil
                              away—no more
                          thoughts, no lead

To the South,
   in the moonlight,
A sash of cloud

                          June—the snow
                              of blossoms
                          On the ground

The mansion of
   the moon
Has hidden faces

                          Ah, the crickets
                              are screaming
                          at the moon

The tree moving
     in the moonlight
Wise to me

                              Middle of my Mandala
                                   —Full moon
                              In the water

At night
     The girl I denied
Walking away

                              My hands on my lap
                                   June night,
                              Full moon

Full moon—
    Pine tree—
Old house

                              Trees cant reach
                                  for a glass
                              Of water

Three little sparrows
    on the roof
Talking quietly, sadly

                              Big books packaged
                                  from Japan—
                              Ritz crackers

The full moon—
  the cat gone—
My sleeping mother

                              Reading the sutra
                                I decided
                              To go straight

One drop from
  the blue spruce—
two more drops

                              Spring moon
                                on 2nd Avenue
                              —girl in white coat

Spring evening—
  hobo with hard on
Like bamboo

Water in the birdbath
    —a film of ice
On the moon

Snow on the grape
  arbor—the little
dead raisins

Buds in the snow
    —the deadly fight
between two birds

Desk cluttered
 with mail—
My mind is quiet

                              Drinking wine
                               —the Queen of Greece
                              on a postage stamp

Playing basketball
 —the lady next door
Watching again

                              New neighbors
                               —light
                              In the old house

Just woke up
    —afternoon pines
Playing the wind.

                              Gray day—
                                the blue spruce
                              Is green

Bach through an open
  dawn window—
the birds are silent

                              Sweet birds, chordless
                                except in another
                              Clime

146

A half a tsphah
  is worse
than none

                          Ah the birds
                            at dawn,
                          my mother and father

Answered a letter
  and took a hot bath
—Spring rain

                          You paid yr homage
                            to the moon,
                          And she sank

147

Sun shining on
 A distant mountain
—the low moon

                              OO a continent
                               in a birdbath—
                              April full moon

Waiting with me for
 the end of this ephemeral
Existence—the moon

                              Pink petals on
                               gnarly Japanese twigs
                              In rain

In the lovely sun
  reading lovely
Haikus—Spring

        Some trees still
          have naked winter look
        —Spring day

Sitting in the sun,
  no bugs yet—
Yellow clover

        My corncob pipe
          hot from
        the sun

The white chair is
    holding its arms out
to Heaven—dandelions

Spring night—
    the neighbor hammering
In the new old house

A bird pecking kernels
 on a grassy hillside
Just mowed

Night—six petals
    have fallen from
Bodhidharma's bouquet

Shooting star!—no,
  lightning bug!—
ah well, June night

                              Lost cat Timmy—
                                he wont be back
                              In a blue moon

After the shower
  my cat meowing
on the porch

                              After the shower
                                the red roses
                              In the green, green

The leaves, fighting
 the empty sky—
No clouds helping

                    The cat musing
                     along the ground—
                    cold gray day

Red roses, white
 clouds, blue sky,
In my birdbath

                    The robin on
                     the television antenna,
                    Something on his beak

Roses! Roses!
  robin wants his
Evening bath!

                    Second thundershower
                      over—the sun
                    Is still high

Worm is looking
  at the moon,
Waiting for me

                    Thunderstorm over
                      —there! The light
                    is on again

My cat's asleep
    —poor little angel,
the burden of flesh!

                        Men and women
                         Yakking beneath
                        the eternal Void

Girl trapped beneath the
    steering wheel, beautiful
As the Dalai Lama's dream

                        The droopy constellation
                         on the grassy hill—
                        Emily Dickinson's Tomb

Am I a flower
  bee, that you
Stare at me?

                        Walking over the water
                          my shadow,
                        Heavier than lead

I woke up
  —two flies were boffing
On my forehead

                        Cool breezy morning
                          —the cat is rolling
                        On his back

Early morning gentle rain,
 two big bumblebees
Humming at their work

                              Summer night—
                               I put out
                              The empty milk bottle

Alone, in old
 clothes, sipping wine
Beneath the moon

                              Autumn eve—my
                               mother playing old
                              Love songs on the piano

Oh another weekend's
  started—people squeaking
On U-turning tires

                          Staring at each other,
                            Squirrel in the branch,
                          Cat in the grass

After the earthquake,
  A child crying
In the silence

                          Little frogs screaming
                            in the ditch
                          At nightfall

After a year and a half
  finally saw the rat,
Big and fat

"The old pond, yes!
  — the water jumped into
By a frog"

Nose hairs in the moon
  —My ass
Is cold

Mexico—After the dim
  markets, bright
San Juan Letran

1960–1966
Northport Haikus

WINTER

Then comes Winter, when I'll be a silent hermit
writing only haiku, like Hardy, or at least haiku-
like quiet last sonatas & conclusive technical spiri-
tual symphonies without youth's anguish.

(Journal)

The sources for these haiku are found in pocket notebooks kept in Northport and Orlando, and in working notebooks dated from 1961 to 1965. In an October 23, 1961, letter to Lawrence Ferlinghetti, Kerouac makes explicit his hope to have him publish a Book of Haikus at City Lights. In early 1964, Kerouac had sent Fernanda Pivano a selection of haiku among other poems for an anthology of American verse to be published in Milan, but had second thoughts about being published in the book. Included too in this section are haiku from another 1964 collection, published posthumously as "Northport Haikus." According to Northport resident and painter Stanley Twardowicz, Kerouac wrote them while the artist did Jack's portrait. These appear to have been written from the point of view of Kerouac's cat, while he was drunk.

Northport Haikus

Two cars passing
 on the freeway
—Husband and wife

October night, lights
 of Connecticut towns
Across the sound

Apassionata Sonata
    —hiballs, gray
Afternoon in October

                 Hot tea, in the cold
                    moonlit snow—
                 a burp

Sunday in a bar
 in Woodland Calif.
—One noon beer

                 Racing westward through
                    the clouds in the howling
                 wind, the moon

The whiteness of the houses
    in the moon
Snow everywhere

                    Windows rattling
                        in the wind
                    I'm a lousy lover

Oh I could drink up
    The whole Yellow River
In my love for Li Po!

                    The falling snow—
                        The hissing radiators—
                    The bride out there

In enormous blizzard
    burying everything
My cat's out mating

In enormous blizzard
    burying everything—
My cat turned back

Spring night—the gleam
    of the fish head eye
In the grass

Too hot to write
    haiku—crickets
and mosquitoes

Sometimes they sleep
   with their lights on,
the June bugs

                     My critics jiggle
                       constantly like
                    Poison ivy in the rain

Dusk now—
   what's left of
An ancient pier

                    Two clouds kissing
                       backed up to look
                    At each other

In the middle of
    the corn, a new
Car slithering

                            Horse waving his tail
                                in a field of clover
                            At sundown

The clouds are
    following each other
Into Eternity

                            Mule on the seashore
                                One thousand foot
                            Bridge above

The bird's still on top
    of that tree,
High above the fog

                        Temple trees
                            across the creek
                        —Fog blowing

One flower
    on the cliffside
Nodding at the canyon

                        A long way from
                            The Beat Generation
                        In the rain forest

Huge knot in the
    Redwood tree
Looking like Zeus' face

                        How cold!—late
                            September baseball—
                        the crickets

Leaves falling everywhere
    in the November
Midnight moonshine

                        Free as a pine
                            goofing
                        For the wind

High in the Sky
    the Fathers Send Messages
From on High

                              Walking on water wasn't
                                  Built in a day

Autumn night
 Salvation Army sign
On a cold brick building

                              Crisp wind
                                  My tired limbs
                              Relaxed before the coals

Spring rain,
    Kicking stones
An arrowhead

                    Winter—that
                        sparrow's nest
                    Still empty

Snow in my shoe
    Abandoned
Sparrow's nest

                    November's New Haven
                        baggagemaster stiffly
                    Disregards my glance

Big drinking & piano
        parties—Christmas
Come and gone—

A current pimple
    In the mind's
Old man

Sleeping on my desk
    head on the sutras,
my cat

The moon is moving,
    thru the clouds
Like a slow balloon

Chou en Lai, his briefcase
    should be fulla leaves,
For all I know

                        And as for Kennedy—
                            in Autumn he slept
                        By swishing peaceful trees

Thanks to Coolidge,
    Hoover—but Autumn,
Roosevelt done America in

                        Everyone of my knocks
                            disturbs my daughter
                        Sleeping in her December grave

Ah Jerusalem—how many
    Autumn saints slaughtered
Thee with Christ?

                    A bird hanging
                        on the wire
                    At dawn

Ah, Genghiz Khan
    weeping—where
did Autumn go?

                    Christ on the Cross crying
                      —his mother missed
                    Her October porridge

The cows of Autumn—
    laughing along the fence,
Roosters at Dawn

                        The son packs
                            quietly as the
                        Mother sleeps

Yellow halfmoon cradled
    among the horizontal boards
Of my fence

                        Frogs don't care
                            just sit there
                        Brooding on the moon

Dawn—the first
　　robins singing
To the new moon

　　　　　　　　　The wind sent
　　　　　　　　　　a leaf on
　　　　　　　　　the robin's back

The carpenter of spring
　　the Zen
of hammer and nail

　　　　　　　　　Spring night
　　　　　　　　　　the silence
　　　　　　　　　Of the stars

Yard tonight an eerie
      moon leafshroud
A midsummernight's dream

                        Haydn's creation or
                              Coleman Hawkins, I can
                        Fix em just right

The racket of the starlings
      in the trees—
My cat's back

                        Ooh! they kicked up
                              a cloud of dust!
                        The birds in my yard

Haiku my eyes!
  my mother is calling!

                    Close your eyes—
                      Landlord knocking
                    On the back door

A quiet Autumn night
  and these fools
Are starting to argue

                    Lonely brickwalls in Detroit
                      Sunday afternoon
                    piss call

O for
   Vermont again—
The barn on an Autumn night

                   Wish I were a rooster
                     and leave my sperm
                 On the sidewalk, shining!

In Hakkaido a cat
  has no luck

                 Every cat in Kyoto
                     can see through the fog

I'll climb up a tree
  and scratch Katapatafataya

                      If I go out now,
                        my paws
                      will get wet

Kneedeep, teeth
  to the blizzard,
My cat gazing at me

                      Kneedeep in the
                        blizzard, the ancient
                      Misery of the cat

Surprising cat fight
   in the parlor on a
Blustery September night

                Rain-in-the-Face
                   looks from the hill:
                Custer down there

Sitting Bull adjusts
   his girdle: the smell
Of smoking fish

The fly, just as
    lonesome as I am
In this empty house

                            The other man, just as
                                lonesome as I am
                            In this empty universe

Notes

I. Book of Haikus

Included in Kerouac's black folder was a letter to a Miss Kupfer-berg; no place or date is given. Included are instructions, as well as a number of haiku: from "The little sparrow" to "Grain elevators, waiting."

"I think these few haikus (Japanese 3-line poems) would be suitable for your purposes because they are eminently simple for children to read or for adults to understand, & yet they are not shallow (as the haiku form demands). . . . p.s. As you may know, haikus always look better 2 or 3 to a page, with drawings, like brush drawings slightly abstract."

Two cars passing   JK NOTE: a rewrite from Buson   EDI-TOR'S NOTE: The travelling pedlar;/Passing each other/On the summer moor.

The windmills of and *Grain elevators, waiting*/—are tall trucks/ —on/—In a 1963 notebook, these are crafted into prose.

Juju beads on   EDITOR'S NOTE: This and "Listen to the birds
     sing"   JK NOTE: °BOOK OF HAIKUS° (collecting them)

In my medicine cabinet   JK NOTE: (with Dody)   EDITOR'S
     NOTE: referring to Dody Muller

The castle of the Gandharvas   EDITOR'S NOTE: Letter to
     Carolyn Cassady, 5/17/54: "We just think that we are dying
     when we die. It is like the castle of the Gandharvas, castles in
     the air . . . a world reflected in a mirror—the end."

Genghis Khan looks fiercely   EDITOR'S NOTE: From 1965:
     "A movie of Genghiz Khan must begin with him wandering
     drunk in the steppes alone, & when he comes to the large
     Mongol camp he just walks into a tent and sits down—turns
     out it's his tent (The Horsemen's guards & scouts followed
     him all night on his drunken pony) . . . "

Chief Crazy Horse   JK NOTE: "my best haiku" Letter to
     Allen Ginsberg and Peter Orlovsky, 12/28/61

*Autumn night in New Haven/—the Whippenpoofers/Singing on
     the train*   EDITOR'S NOTE: Inside the back jacket of the
     Avon paperback of Henry Miller's *The Air-Conditioned Night-
     mare* owned by Kerouac is the following in pencil: Autumn

night/The conductors getting/Drunk in the ladies room, and Autumn night/boisterous conductor/Bottle in hand.

A turtle sailing along   EDITOR'S NOTE: This and following, "A black bull" and "Catfish fighting for his life" are taken from this 1961 notebook with   JK NOTE: HAIKUS ON THE ST. JOHN'S RIVER (SITUATIONS)

The poppies!—   JK NOTE: HAIKU
"The poppy flowers
How calmly
They fell."   —ETSUJIN (I could die in delicacy now)

Hurrying things along,   Letter to Lawrence Ferlinghetti, 10/23/61   JK NOTE: "Or a BOOK OF HAIKUS with my drawings, like this, see (casual, Karumi-lightness)"   EDITOR'S NOTE: [wanted him to publish Book of Haikus]

That's an unencouraging sign,   JK NOTE: (dream) [var. That's an encouraging sign]

Following each other,   EDITOR'S NOTE: In letter to Allen following "that whole B[lack] M[ountain] gang is full of shit . . ."

Run over by my lawnmower,   JK NOTE: "What wd Bashō say if he knew Jack Kerouac's lawnmower ran over a frog? /

(He was just pushed—in tangled turf—not cut, or crusht, or anything)/I ran over that frog, I decided to go live in the woods and leave things as they are, among the animals,— lawns indeed!"

The summer chair   EDITOR'S NOTE: See Shiki: "Nobody there;/A wicker chair in the shade;/Fallen pine needles"

A full November moon/   [var. Maggie Cassidy], Kerouac's fictive name for Mary Carney

Spring night—the sound   JK NOTE: "Doesn't that make you feel spring? fresh fish heads, too. You shoulda heard him chlomp the eyes"

A big fat flake   JK NOTE: Letter to Lois Sorrells "And just now as I was pondering your new poem idea I SAW a haiku out the window"

A long island   JK NOTE: "Now, the American Haiku—Haiku is a 'world of meaning in a miniature,' as Blyth says"

Like: "White dew—
        over the potato field,
The Milky Way"   —Shiki

Barley soup in Scotland   EDITOR'S NOTE: Blyth notes that
  "barley's autumn is summer" in that farmers are cutting,
  thrashing, and stacking, an image of health and vitality, a con-
  trast to misery.

II. Dharma Pops

Tathagata neither loathes   refers to the immutable and im-
  movable in all things

Walking along the night beach,   JK NOTE: "took night walk
  on beach with wine—the music included wild Arabic bag-
  pipes high and far out, quite unlike Scot bagpipes" (Tangier)

Shall I say no?   EDITOR'S NOTE: See Issa's "oh, don't swat/
  the fly rubs hands/rubs feet"

III. 1956: Desolation Pops SPRING

Poor tortured teeth   JK NOTE: "(haiku thought on road with
  ride I got from JCity, to clear to Portland, little blond Jack
  Fitzgerald painter with spattered shoes & 4 cans of cold pint

beer, we drank em & had another in a tavern with sweet sincere bartender)"

Aurora Borealis/over Hozomeen—   JK NOTE: Haiku for Gary

Late afternoon—   EDITOR'S NOTE: prose sequence in *Dharma Bums*

Wednesday blah   EDITOR'S NOTE: See Chapter 34 of *Dharma Bums,* final paragraph: "I added 'Blah,' with a little grin, because I knew that shack and that mountain would understand . . ."

Skhandas my ass!   refers to birth, old age, death, duration, and change.

I called—Dipankara   legendary Buddha preceding historical one.

Nirvana, as when the rain   JK NOTE TO ROBERT LAX, 10/26/54: "That's what nirvana means NIRVIA (blown out), state of being blown out, state of being completely extinguished."

I Notes *I*

IV. 1957: Road Haikus SUMMER

*Three pencils arranged, . . . Sambaghakaya, Nirvanakaya, Dhar-
   makaya*   represent the three bodies possessed by Buddha

The wind agrees with me   JK NOTE: "(a very lazy fine drowsy
   haiku)"

The barking dog—   JK NOTE: "(crazy haiku, lunatic haiku)"

Hand in hand in a red valley   With "The first morning—hand
   in hand/With the universal schoolteacher/in a red valley" Ker-
   ouac concludes: "Haikus shd be spontaneous above all, so I
   take first version"—Thurs April 4, 1957

Lonesome blubbers   JK NOTE: "(crooners on radio)"

The jazz trombone,   JK NOTE: speaking of "greenish" dig a
   great haiku by Buson: "The flowers of the persimmon;/those
   which fell yesterday/Look yellowish"

Here comes/My dragon—/goodbye!   Letter to Peter and Allen
   and Bill, 6/7/57   JK NOTE: "Myself I am now reading the
   FULL TRANSLATION of the Lanka Vatara Scripture which

is enlightening me for good now, by Suzuki, and I just read the Book of Chinese Immortals all about ancient Chinese sages who were junkies on Gold juice and Cinnabar and after they died people would only find a shoe in their grave and suddenly overhead there they go on a dragon . . . never die!"

The backyard I tried to draw   JK NOTE: or, even better, by Buson, "The nightingale is singing,/Its small mouth/Open"

The son who wants solitude,   JK NOTE: "(which I just wrote) maybe a haiku, but the reason why I dunno—(Perhaps only <u>sounds</u> like a haiku)—"

On the sidewalk/A dead baby bird   Letter to Peter, Allen, Bill, 6/7/57   JK NOTE:

Nuerishi de	(This sparrow hops
Suzuma no hariku	Along the veranda,
Roka Kana	With wet feet) (Shiki)

How that butterfly'll wake up   EDITOR'S NOTE: haiku parody, see Buson's "On the hanging bell/Has perched and is fast asleep,/A butterfly!"

Buddha laughing   Letter to Peter, Allen, Bill, 6/7/57: "A senryu parody (everybody IS in the act—JK).

V. 1958–1959 Beat Generation Haikus AUTUMN

Autumnal cowflops—a man [variation: but a man]   EDITOR'S
   NOTE: Kerouac may have been responding to J. Donald
   Adams in his "Speaking of Books" column of the May 18, 1958,
   New York Times where Adams opined that "Beat Generation"
   should be renamed "bleat generation," since "bleating is a
   monotonous sound. . . . and I think the writings of this group
   are more effective [as a sleep inducer] than the long-recom-
   mended prescription of counting silent sheep as they jump
   over a stile." Hence Kerouac's barnyard imagery.

Fall trees—   [from scroll ms. "On the Beat Generation" 6 Nov.
   1958]   JK NOTE: "(a Beat generation haiku)"

Middle of my Mandala   Mandala is a circle, a representation
   of cosmic forces.

Trees cant reach   Letter to Philip Whalen, June 12, 1958: "I
   think American Haikus shd. never have more than 3 words a
   line . . ."

Three little sparrows   Letter to Philip Whalen, early Nov. '58:
   "Then he [DT Suzuki] said, 'You young men sit here quietly

and write haikus while I go and make some powdered green
tea' . . . I wrote a haiku for him:"

A half a tsphah   JK NOTE: "Paul Bowles haiku"

You paid yr homage   JK NOTE: "To my cat: (out at night):—"

Night—six petals   Bodhidharma is a Buddhist patriarch and
teacher of the 5th–6th century.

Girl trapped beneath the   Dalai Lama is a teacher, a symbol
of reincarnation.

The droopy constellation   EDITOR'S NOTE: Letter to Philip
Whalen, 1/16/56: "Haiku is nice but it's small, I mean, there
are a million haikus in one good prose work and a million
haikus in the Great Emily Dickinson too—that rhyme even!"

Alone, in old   JK NOTE: "a series of incoherent drunken haiku"

After the earthquake,   JK NOTE: "(Mexico City earthquake
1957)"

"The old pond, yes!   JK NOTE: —Bashō, my transliteration.
EDITOR'S NOTE: See "Runover by my lawnmower"; and
One Hundred Frogs by Hiroaki Sato

VI. 1960–1966 Northport Haikus WINTER

Free as a pine   Letter to Philip Whalen, 3/15/59: "You're the only one who never yelled at me 'for drinking too much' . . . "

Walking on water wasn't   JK NOTE: "(said I on mushrooms)" EDITOR'S NOTE: Allen Ginsberg suggested Jack try Timothy Leary's experiments with psychedelics in the early sixties. This line was one result.

THE WIND SENT   JK NOTE: "Realized today I can write better haikus by considering the haiku situation in French first—" THUS:—   EDITOR'S NOTE: See also Bashō's "Sticking on the mushroom/The leaf/Of some unknown tree"

Ooh! they kicked up   JK NOTE: "[a series of incoherent drunken haiku]"

The other man, just as   EDITOR'S NOTE: See Bashō's "Turn this way;/I also am lonely,/This evening of autumn"

Haiku Sources

UNPUBLISHED MATERIAL

Book of Haikus, folder
Pocket Notebooks, date indicated where possible
"Desolation Pops 1956" (unpublished manuscript)
"On the Beat Generation," Nov. 6, 1958 (scroll manuscript)
"Beat Generation Haikus," essay ms., Rare Books and Manuscripts Library, Columbia University
"Old Angel Midnight/Lucien Midnight" manuscript, 1957 Berg Collection, New York Public Library
"Northport Haikus" (printed pamphlet, Beat Sun Press, 1964)
Working Notebooks 1961–1965, Berg Collection, New York Public Library

LETTERS (PUBLISHED AND UNPUBLISHED)

Selected Letters 1940–1956, ed. Ann Charters, New York: Viking, 1995
Selected Letters 1957–1969, ed. Ann Charters, New York: Viking, 1999

⟦ Haiku Sources ⟧

Letter to Peter Orlovsky, Allen Ginsberg, Bill Burroughs, 6/7/57, Ginsberg Collection, Rare Books and Manuscripts Library, Columbia University

Letter to Joyce Johnson, June 11, 1957, *Door Wide Open,* New York: Viking, 2000

Letter to Gary Snyder, 1/12/58, Gary Snyder Collected Letters, University of California, Davis

Postcards to Allen Ginsberg, 4/5/59 and 6/2/60, Rare Books and Manuscripts Library, Columbia University

Letters to Peter Orlovsky, March 23 and April 1960, Rare Books and Manuscripts Library, Columbia University

BOOKS (LISTED IN ORDER OF COMPOSITION)

Maggie Cassidy [early 1953], New York: Avon, 1959

Some of the Dharma [December 1953–March 15, 1956], New York: Viking, 1997

Desolation Angels [1956, 1961], New York: Putnam, 1965

Dharma Bums [November 1957], New York: Viking, 1958

Heaven & Other Poems, Bolinas, California: Grey Fox, 1959

Trip Trap: Haiku along the Road from San Francisco to New York: 1959 (with Albert Saijo and Lew Welch), Bolinas, California: Grey Fox, 1973

Lonesome Traveler [1960], New York: McGraw-Hill, 1960

Big Sur [October 1961], New York: Farrar, Straus, Cudahy, 1962

I Haiku Sources *I*

Scattered Poems, compiled by Ann Charters, San Francisco: City
    Lights, 1971
Pomes All Sizes, San Francisco: City Lights, 1992 [Manuscripts
    in Berg Collection, New York Public Library]

RECORDING

American Haikus from *Blues & Haikus* recording, [1959], Rhino
    Word Beat, 1990

Selected Bibliography

Agostini, Bertrand, and Christiane Pajotin. *Itineraire dans l'errance, Jack Kerouac et le haiku.* Grigny: Editions Paroles D'Aube, 1998.

Blyth, R. H. *Haiku.* 4 vols. Tokyo: Hokuseido Press, 1949–52.

———. *Senryu: Japanese Satirical Verses.* Tokyo: Hokuseido Press, 1949.

———. *A History of Haiku.* 2 vols. Tokyo: Hokuseido Press, 1963–64.

Fields, Rick. *How the Swans Came to the Lake: A Narrative History of Buddhism in America.* Boston & London: Shambhala, 1992.

Ginsberg, Allen. "Review of The Dharma Bums." *The Village Voice,* November 12, 1958, pp. 3–5.

———. "Paris Review Interview." *Beat Writers at Work.* Edited by George Plimpton. New York: Modern Library, 1999. pp. 31–68.

Goddard, Dwight, ed. *A Buddhist Bible.* Boston: Beacon, 1938.

Henderson, Harold G. *An Introduction to Haiku: An Anthology of Poems and Poets from Bashō to Shiki.* Garden City: Doubleday, Anchor, 1958.

Kerouac, Jack. "Paris Review Interview." *Beat Writers at Work.* Edited by George Plimpton. New York: Modern Library, 1999. pp. 97–133.

———. "The Origins of Joy in Poetry." *Good Blonde & Others.* Edited by Donald Allen. San Francisco: Grey Fox, 1993. p. 74.

———. *Visions of Cody.* New York: McGraw-Hill, 1972.

————. *Doctor Sax.* New York: Grove, 1959.

Lynch, Tom. "'A path toward nature': Haiku's Aesthetics of Awareness." *Literature of Nature: An International Sourcebook.* Edited by Patrick D. Murphy. Chicago, London: Fitzroy Dearborn, 1998. pp. 116–25.

————. "A Way of Awareness: The Emerging Delineaments of American Haiku" (unpublished essay).

————. *An Original Relation to the Universe: Emersonian Poetics of Immanence and Contemporary American Haiku* (unpublished doctoral dissertation, June 1989).

Pizzarelli, Alan. "Spontaneous Notes on the Haiku and Related Poetic Forms of Jack Kerouac" (unpublished essay).

Sato, Hiroaki. "Senryu vs. Haiku." Essay written for the Haiku Society of America. December 11, 1993.

————. *One Hundred Frogs.* New York: Weatherhill, 1995.

Shirane, Haruo. *Traces of Dreams: Landscapes, Cultural Memory, and the Poetry of Bashō.* Stanford, Calif.: Stanford University Press, 1998.

Snyder, Gary. *The Gary Snyder Reader: Prose, Poetry, and Translations, 1952–1998.* Washington, D.C.: Counterpoint, 1999.

Tonkinson, Carole, ed. *Big Sky Mind: Buddhism and the Beat Generation.* New York: Riverhead, 1995.

Ungar, Barbara. *Haiku in English.* Stanford, Calif.: Stanford Honors Essay in Humanities Number XXI, 1978.

van den Heuvel, Cor, ed. *The Haiku Anthology.* New York: Norton, 1999.